CRAP CYCLE LANES

CRAP CYCLE LANES

Crap Cycle Lanes

Published by Eye Books Ltd 2007
8 Peacock Yard
Iliffe Street
London
SE17 3LH

Tel. +44 (0) 845 450 8870
www.eye-books.com

Typeset in Helvetica

ISBN-10: 1-903-070-589
ISBN-13: 978-1903-070-581

This book was inspired by the "Facility of the Month" feature on the
Warrington Cycle Campaign website.

Copyright 2007 Warrington Cycle Campaign.
Design by David Whelan for Eye Books.

Printed and bound in Malta by Gutenberg Press

eye**Opener**

We publish a number of books on cycling, and this is more coincidence than planning. And it seems that many of the facilities featured in this book have come about by the same process. Their inclusion in the 1st edition of Crap Cycle Lanes is not coincidence, though. We're sure that they deserve their places here.

Our books champion people who are living as opposed to simply existing. We want to celebrate that ordinary people can and do extraordinary things – it seems that many people are taking on extraordinary journeys by bike.

This over time has subconsciously lifted both interest and awareness of cycling to all linked with Eye. Through this we have been made aware of the various active cycling campaigns around the country and came across Warrington Cycle Campaign. Their world renowned "Facility of the month" feature inspired this book. We feel proud of our association with them and support the important message they campaign for.

Dan Hiscocks
Founder and Publisher
eye books
Challenging the way we see things

A WORD FROM
WARRINGTON CYCLE CAMPAIGN

In 2001 Warrington Cycle Campaign member Pete Owens decided that there was cause for concern with a cycle path around a large roundabout in Warrington which had many obstructions. Here was a cycle path created by white lining a stretch of pavement with no consideration as to whether it was actually able to be cycled around. Most obviously there was a litter bin which forced cyclists out next to the cars on the road passing in the opposite direction. He therefore displayed it on the Campaign's website.

The idea was used for other notorious cycle "farcilities" which started to accumulate, each with a "pithy" humorous comment from Pete. This then turned into the "Facility of The Month" page. Soon the entries were noticed by other cycle campaigners throughout the country who sent in their own examples of local designs.

Awareness of Pete's work grew and web hits were soon being received from around the world. WCC's website became a global resource for showing poor design and practice.

In 2006 the national papers picked up on the existence of the website when changes were being considered to the Highway Code regarding the use of cycle facilities.

In October 2007 WCC presented at a Cycle Forum in New York being hosted by the New Yorker magazine.

Warrington Cycle Campaign have been very successful in blending the humorous pictures of "dodgy" cycle facilities with the very serious need to change the way politicians and those in government provide a better environment to promote cycling as an alternative to car use. The "Facility Of The Month" site shows quite graphically how the idea that you can effectively promote cycling with "token" cycle paths, lanes and facilities is flawed.

So many of our cycle facilities in this country are simply ludicrous. WCC believe that on balance cycle facilities in the UK make little real difference to cycle safety or convenience and at worst are very dangerous. Far better results would come from sensibly sharing the roads for motor vehicles, cyclists and pedestrians with a 20 mph speed limit in all residential and urban areas. This works in so many countries in Northern Europe where cities, towns and villages have far higher levels of cycling and pedestrian safety.

Finally, we must acknowledge the efforts of the traffic and highway engineers in local authorities around the country. Without their lack of forethought, lack of design skills, or simple mindedness then this publication would not have been possible.

And if you want to see even newer examples then please visit our website at:

www.warringtoncyclecampaign.co.uk

CRAP CYCLE LANES

THE BLUNT END

If the light shows red, one should presumably wait, before dismounting.

Of course, if the light is green, any cyclist dull-witted enough to ignore the directions would find their bike much more closely resembling the shape painted on the pavement. They'd also gain a pole-shaped memorial dink in the centre of their bonce.

DIFFICULTY

The oval wheels of the stylised, pedal-less bike poise thrillingly below the 'END' motif, for which a native Greek- or Russian-speaking signwriter has been painstakingly sought out.

DANGER LEVEL

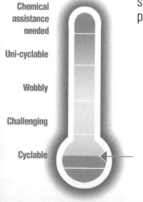

Chemical assistance needed

Uni-cyclable

Wobbly

Challenging

Cyclable

Just about safe

Hazardous

Scary

Life threatening

F**** ME!!!!

Sentencing recommendation:

The misplaced creativity alone should earn the council officers responsible for this muppetry a CAUTION. And 3 points on their poetic license.

CAUTION

HEAD-ON SLALOM

A splendid vantage from which to enjoy the thumping of an oncoming dual carriageway. Note how cheekily the dashed 'STOP' lines tease the edge of a downhill slope, themselves slanting deceptively.

The footpath grip and the decorated black bollard combine to offer poignant distractions to the rider's right, taking their attention pleasingly away from the dull rumble of vehicles bearing down upon him, or her, from the fore.

See also, how the rider is beckoned on by the minute strip of cyclepath, just the other side of where the traffic has been directed to joust with them for sport.

DIFFICULTY

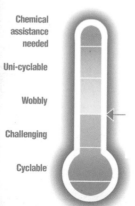

Chemical
assistance
needed

Uni-cyclable

Wobbly

Challenging

Cyclable

DANGER LEVEL

Just about safe

Hazardous

Scary

Life threatening

F**** ME!!!!

Sentencing recommendation:

Salisbury City Council's manic double-thinking richly deserves our recommendation of TAGGING AND A CURFEW.

CRAP CYCLE LANES

THE (brief) RED CARPET TREATMENT

CRAP CYCLE LANES

No expense of public money has been spared in these several meters of luxurious cycling Nirvana. Notice the generous stopping distance afforded for titanium-thighed Stratford-Upon-Avon bicycle titans, who may reach escape velocity in the first turn of the pedal.

The concrete bollard, perfectly placed to assure that the pavement remains impeccably useless, does double duty as a handy leaning post. Riders can use it to lean against, to recover from the exhilaration that this spectacular ride is bound to produce.

DIFFICULTY

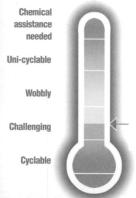

Chemical assistance needed

Uni-cyclable

Wobbly

Challenging

Cyclable

DANGER LEVEL

Just about safe

Hazardous

Scary

Life threatening

F**** ME!!!!

Sentencing recommendation:

For the planners, planning meetings, competitive tendering, and sheer work effort which produced this inane whimsy, expressed in tarmac, we propose an ASBO.

CRAP CYCLE LANES

CRAP CYCLE LANES

The Liverpool Street area of the City of London affords a tantalising little tease of a bike lane. Now it's a bike lane, now it's not. Or perhaps the City of London wants to encourage people to *bring* bicycles to Finsbury Circus, but then to make a stately procession, pushing the bike along the cycle path, for which the pavement has been so expensively widened.

Did they have a change of heart? Or has this stretch earned a fearsome reputation as a wobbling blackspot? Or is this a cycle path on every day that has a 'T' in its name, but not on days with a 'U' in, leaving Mondays, Wednesdays and Fridays to float, with the phases of the moon, perhaps?

We have a right to know.

DIFFICULTY

Chemical assistance needed

Uni-cyclable

Wobbly

Challenging

Cyclable

DANGER LEVEL

Just about safe

Hazardous

Scary

Life threatening

F**** ME!!!!

Sentencing recommendation:

The City of London spends, what, a tenner at least, putting down a cycle lane, then arbitrarily revokes it with an ink-jet printed A4 page, held up with nylon cable-ties. Reprehensible. We recommend a CAUTION

CAUTION

CRAP CYCLE LANES

GIVE WAY - OR ELSE

Here is a sign which not only tells you to give way, but enforces an on-the-spot sanction, should you be slow to comply. As the trucks and the 70mph speed limit signs show, along with the casual scattering of traffic cones, this is a great spot for recreational cycling.

Everybody has a responsibility for road safety, and it is not something to be taken lightly under any circumstances. Decapitation seems a little harsh though.

Richard Brunstrom, the Chief Constable of North Wales has described this portion of Route 5 of the Sustrans National Cycle Network as 'a disaster waiting to happen.'

DIFFICULTY

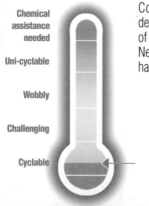

Chemical assistance needed

Uni-cyclable

Wobbly

Challenging

Cyclable

DANGER LEVEL

Just about safe

Hazardous

Scary

Life threatening

F**** ME!!!!

Sentencing recommendation:

This is about as hazardous as a cycle track could be. You wouldn't be much more at risk slip-streaming with the trucks on their way to Holyhead. Definitely a case for REGIME CHANGE.

REGIME CHANGE

CRAP CYCLE LANES

SIZE DOES MATTER IN READING

We do like to see a nice spruce, colourful cycle lane. Reading has certainly gone beyond the call of duty in providing a bright green grip-strip, lovely, vivid double yellows and cycle-lane markings in a pristine white that a toothpaste ad could drool over.

All of this attention to detail and sheer craft is refreshing. It means that there is no chance whatsoever of even the most inattentive cyclist missing the start of this beautiful facility.

DIFFICULTY Nor would they miss its perfectly presented end, at least 20 vibrant yards along the road. **DANGER LEVEL**

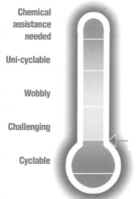

Chemical assistance needed

Uni-cyclable

Wobbly

Challenging

Cyclable

Just about safe

Hazardous

Scary

Life threatening

F***** ME!!!!

Sentencing recommendation:

This is hardly a hanging offense. unless you pay council tax in Reading, of course, then you might take a more stern view of this half-baked street decor. Assuming this is a first offense, we recommend a CAUTION.

CAUTION

NOSTALIGIA'S NOT WHAT IT WAS

CRAP CYCLE LANES

Ah, it does my heart good to see. Forgive me the indulgence, I know that the sight of a red Routemaster means little or nothing to those who live outside of St Kensberg, but it makes my breath give a little quiver.

"Only a ghastly dehumanised moron would want to get rid of the Routemaster," said Ken Livingstone in 2001. We don't agree about much, Ken and I, but we're solid on that.

DIFFICULTY

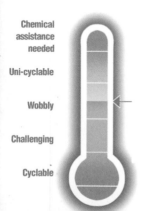

Chemical assistance needed

Uni-cyclable

Wobbly

Challenging

Cyclable

Sorry – the bike lane... toddle along the Red Route, where you can play 'keep your wheels between the red lines,' make a 90° turn in about a meter, then see if you can screech a stop before you get one eye each side of the traffic light pole, and your teeth embedded in the pedestrian placebo-box.

DANGER LEVEL

Just about safe

Hazardous

Scary

Life threatening

F**** ME!!!!

Sentencing recommendation:

Hanging's too good for – I'm sorry, – I'm back on the Routemaster. This is moronic. Ghastly, dehumanised and moronic. Our recommendation: REGIME CHANGE.

REGIME CHANGE

OFF-ROAD ON-ROAD

Far too few cyclists take the time and trouble to practice their slalom and BMX skills. Colchester City Council have taken a modest-looking but pro-active approach to the problem, providing this simple obstacle course.

Local car drivers selflessly contribute daily variation by parking randomly all over the bike lane.

DIFFICULTY

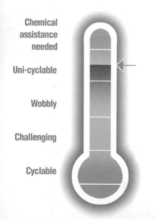

Chemical assistance needed

Uni-cyclable

Wobbly

Challenging

Cyclable

DANGER LEVEL

Just about safe

Hazardous

Scary

Life threatening

F**** ME!!!!

Sentencing recommendation:

This complete lack of care and attention, in our view, merited an ASBO, but this was reduced to a CAUTION on appeal.

CAUTION

OAPs THRILL-RIDE

CRAP CYCLE LANES

A thoughtful offering as a distraction on the promenade. Not only is there a great opportunity to slam into an iron barricade at the bottom, but also a chance to mingle with pedestrians at the top, who can reach the steps only by crossing the cycle path.

Good thinking on Clacton's part, since the average age of pedestrians is often in the high 70s and above.

DIFFICULTY

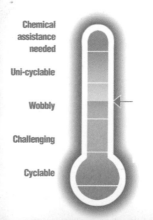

Chemical assistance needed

Uni-cyclable

Wobbly

Challenging

Cyclable

DANGER LEVEL

Just about safe

Hazardous

Scary

Life threatening

F***** ME!!!!

Sentencing recommendation:

Obviously, Clacton couldn't have sprung for a concrete ramp. That would have been way too expensive. For their penny-pinching half wittedness, we propose Clacton planners be awarded - TAGGING AND A CURFEW

TAG AND CURFEW

CRAP CYCLE LANES

CAMBRIDGESHIRE
– CYCLING CAPITAL OF THE FENS

Doesn't it restore your faith in humanity to think of the effort they must have given to go through all the bureaucracy and hurdles of budget appropriation to provide this delightful, scenic cyclepath, several bike lengths long.

The track takes intrepid riders from precisely nowhere, all the way to a drain and a drive, exactly nowhere else, taking in a veritable sliver of sights along the main freight road to the coast and Felixstowe docks. The picture doesn't quite do the council justice, since there is an almost identical path on the other side, so that, after you've recovered from the thrill of the ride, you can enjoy it again in the opposite direction.

DIFFICULTY

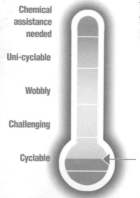

Chemical assistance needed

Uni-cyclable

Wobbly

Challenging

Cyclable

DANGER LEVEL

Just about safe

Hazardous

Scary

Life threatening

F***** ME!!!!

Sentencing recommendation:

If this is an example of Cambridgeshire's commitment to carbon-free travel (and other entries in this book suggest that it is), then a CUSTODIAL SENTENCE is richly deserved.

CRAP CYCLE LANES

SALUBRIOUS SLIDEWAY

We may have Network Rail to thank for this bike-slide. A 180° turn on the other side means that it's really only fun to ride the rail coming this way.

Still, between avoiding the handrail and jostling with pedestrians, the cycle facility certainly presents an invigorating challenge on the way to work.

DIFFICULTY

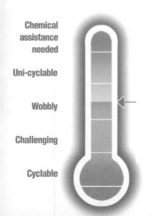

Chemical assistance needed

Uni-cyclable

Wobbly

Challenging

Cyclable

DANGER LEVEL

Just about safe

Hazardous

Scary

Life threatening

F**** ME!!!!

Sentencing recommendation:

These rails are a scream as long as nothing exciting happens. If it does, they are, obviously, lethal. We would recommend REGIME CHANGE, although we aren't able to ascertain which regime the shock'n'order should be addressed to.

REGIME CHANGE

POLICE PROTECTION

Pimlico's finest provide an excellent illustration of how well these bike lanes amalgamate with parking bays and the popular 90s traffic calming corrugated kerbs.

How nice of our boys in blue to make sure nobody parks illegally in the bike lane, by occupying it themselves.

DIFFICULTY

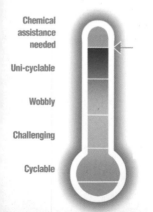

Chemical assistance needed

Uni-cyclable

Wobbly

Challenging

Cyclable

DANGER LEVEL

Just about safe

Hazardous

Scary

Life threatening

F**** ME!!!!

Sentencing recommendation:

Although entertaining, the fashion for weaving cycle lanes through traffic puzzles is hazardous, as well as bafflingly unpredictable. This wooden-headed approach to cycle facility provision would probably merit TAGGING & CURFEW if it weren't in our congested capital city. With that in mind, we strongly recommend for the City of Westminster; REGIME CHANGE

CRAP CYCLE LANES

CRAWLEY

We can only wonder what motivated Crawley planners in this delightful initiative. A cycle lane that stretches out across a traffic lane, abruptly ending about a meter from the kerb. the idea is, presumably, to stop by the 'END' marking, then lift or push the bicycle the last two and a half feet.

It's easy to imagine the patient smiles as happy drivers await the completion of this inexplicable ritual.

DIFFICULTY

Chemical
assistance
needed

Uni-cyclable

Wobbly

Challenging

Cyclable

DANGER LEVEL

Just about safe

Hazardous

Scary

Life threatening

F**** ME!!!!

Sentencing recommendation:

What sequence of proposals, negotiation and planning can have given rise to this street furniture farce. The bizarre 'thinking' that produced this biker-baffler can surely only be rewarded with TAGGING AND A CURFEW

A PRESTON PUZZLE

Perhaps with a limited tarmac budget for cycle lanes, Preston Highways Department reasoned that, by making them narrower, they could stretch them farther along.

Perhaps the town planner is a slow cyclist, with a pathological loathing of being overtaken. Or perhaps the plan had only the route indicated, and a pedantic contractor scaled up the line on the map. Or maybe it's a course carefully designed to test whether the cyclist's morning dose of caffeine is sufficient.

Whatever it is, it's an eminently worthy entry for Crap Cycle Lanes.

DIFFICULTY

Chemical assistance needed

Uni-cyclable

Wobbly

Challenging

Cyclable

DANGER LEVEL

Just about safe

Hazardous

Scary

Life threatening

F**** ME!!!!

Sentencing recommendation:

This track must have been built either to test or to torture users. Either way, it should certainly earn North Preston highways commissioners a CAUTION

CAUTION

CRAP CYCLE LANES

CUNNING STUNTS

CRAP CYCLE LANES

Stockport's little cycling confection packs an astonishing range of action into a very compact space. This has something for everybody. After you've hopped up onto the pavement, there's a swift chicane around a signpost and a whimsical bollard which serves no purpose other than to present a hazard.

The giddying meter-and-a-half of free cycling straight leads to where a calm, gentle slope brings you to a stop, right by the path of a motorist.

And this is not just any motorist, this motorist has just been infuriated by a dodgem-test of their own. This cycle path manages to be useless, baffling and dangerous, all in less than six bike lengths.

It is a nice green, though, isn't it.

DIFFICULTY

Chemical assistance needed

Uni-cyclable

Wobbly

Challenging

Cyclable

DANGER LEVEL

Just about safe

Hazardous

Scary

Life threatening

F**** ME!!!!

Sentencing recommendation:

Just look at what was at this corner before
inspiration descended upon the local planning
department; a pavement wide enough for
pedestrians, and a road wide enough for traffic.
Look at the mess that it's in now. People get
paid for this kind of thing, and they get paid
from the residents coffers. we recommend a
CUSTODIAL SENTENCE

HUMAN FROGGER

This provides a thrilling chicane, on which to catapult oneself from, then suddenly back into, the traffic.

Stockport also seem to believe that, where cycle lanes are concerned, less is more. Or perhaps this is a carefully considered anger-management scheme for pedestrians; ensuring that people crossing the road can be separately inconvenienced by cyclists and drivers.

DIFFICULTY

DANGER LEVEL

Perhaps Stockport should exlend this idea, and segregate more lanes. Lanes where pedestrians can wait first for cyclists to pass, then cars, then buses, and last of all lorries.

Then, of course they'd be in the middle of the road, so they would have to wait for lorries and trucks going the other way, then the buses, then cars and then bicycles, all over again. Splendid.

Chemical assistance needed

Uni-cyclable

Wobbly

Challenging

Cyclable

Just about safe

Hazardous

Scary

Life threatening

F**** ME!!!

Sentencing recommendation:

Remedial education is about the only thing we can think of to help this mentally impoverished council, but in the format, we'd have to recommend an ASBO

CRAP CYCLE LANES

NO THROUGH TRAFFIC

CRAP CYCLE LANES

One thing that we can be thankful for is that oncoming vehicles pose very little danger to cyclists here.

The hazard on this cycle lane comes from cars parked outside peoples houses.

Now, who could have predicted that?

DIFFICULTY

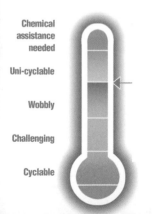

- Chemical assistance needed
- Uni-cyclable
- Wobbly
- Challenging
- Cyclable

DANGER LEVEL

- Just about safe
- Hazardous
- Scary
- Life threatening
- F***** ME!!!!

Sentencing recommendation:

There is only one thing for Lancaster District Council. The only way they'll learn to consider cyclists when they're planning cycle paths is an extended period of TAGGING AND A CURFEW

THE JIG

CRAP CYCLE LANES

Haxby Road in York has a cycle path that follows an increasingly popular trend for cycle-calming measures.

Coming as they do right after a crank in the tightly-fenced path, they add to the delicious box of surprises that are available to both pedestrians and cyclists alike.

They also ensure that cyclists following this route for the first time can form an intimate and maybe indivisible union between their handlebars and their own most tender parts.

DIFFICULTY

DANGER LEVEL

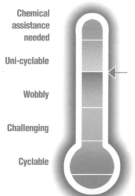

Chemical assistance needed

Uni-cyclable

Wobbly

Challenging

Cyclable

Just about safe

Hazardous

Scary

Life threatening

F**** ME!!!!

Sentencing recommendation:

York City Council highways department really out to have their goolies mashed for this, or at the least, a few days in the stocks, but we can only recommend a CUSTODIAL SENTENCE

CRAP CYCLE LANES

WAPPING WHEELIES

A tiny masterpiece. This bike lane is just the right shape and size to target when you materialise your bike-TARDIS, landing on end, squarely in the middle of the carriageway.

Imagine the surprise on the nouveaux-cockney faces of drivers on their way to work. Seriously; what are cyclists really supposed to do here? Uni-cycle the perimeter? Pop endless rotating wheelies?

DIFFICULTY

Chemical
assistance
needed

Uni-cyclable

Wobbly

Challenging

Cyclable

DANGER LEVEL

Just about safe

Hazardous

Scary

Life threatening

F**** ME!!!

Sentencing recommendation:

Tower Hamlets must have been struggling to meet some kind of a target with this bike lane, but the target is too small to be of any use to a cyclist. We recommend a CUSTODIAL SENTENCE.

FOR (VERY) SKINNY OFF-ROADERS

CRAP CYCLE LANES

The arcane motives behind these genius examples of cycle facility is a mystery that would fox Inspector Rebus. A disappearing half of a cyclepath, a track so narrow that you'd struggle to carry your bike aloft and, best of all, a cycle lane leading right into a fence, with a drop to a car-park entrance ramp on the other side.

Really – does that unprepossessing fence actually represent such a superb starting point for a tour of the Royal Borough that they expect us to carry our bikes to the fence, or are we missing the obvious, magical allure that this fence holds as a destination?

DIFFICULTY

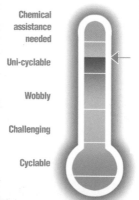

Chemical assistance needed

Uni-cyclable

Wobbly

Challenging

Cyclable

DANGER LEVEL

Just about safe

Hazardous

Scary

Life threatening

F**** ME!!!!

Sentencing recommendation:

Either Edinburgh Council mean well, but are cognitively challenged, or they just don't give a stuff, and they don't care who knows it. Whichever, they really need some kind of a sanction that will get their attention. we recommend a CUSTODIAL SENTENCE

CRAP CYCLE LANES

TOO CLOSE TO CALL

CRAP CYCLE LANES

Quite quick traffic trucks along this route. The long arrow seems to hint at the imperative for cycles to get a move on, as well as helpfully instructing riders on the direction of travel.

What options one should then choose, from the far end of this 3 meter marvel, (insofar as the end to such a brief sojourn could correctly be called 'far'), the signage neglects to indicate.

DIFFICULTY

Given the pace and proximity of passing Peugeots, some deft manoeuvring is certainly required both at the start and at the end.

DANGER LEVEL

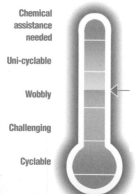

Chemical assistance needed

Uni-cyclable

Wobbly

Challenging

Cyclable

Just about safe

Hazardous

Scary

Life threatening

F**** ME!!!!

Sentencing recommendation:

What to recommend? If it's just this time, a CAUTION. But if it happens again, it will have to be REGIME CHANGE.

RUTTING SEASON

CRAP CYCLE LANES

Every cyclist likes a challenge. If we didn't, we wouldn't set out to joust with juggernauts every day on the way to work. We stare down speeding Scanias before breakfast, no worry.

This cycle facility is just the sort of thing that can make the daily commute a perennial well-spring of joy; a ragged, drain-pitted tyre-grabbing rut, flanked by half-awake drivers ready to slough out from the row of sleepy parking spaces to the left, with a nice straight road roaring on the right.

DIFFICULTY

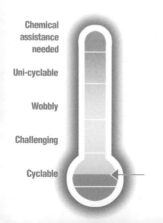

Chemical
assistance
needed

Uni-cyclable

Wobbly

Challenging

Cyclable

DANGER LEVEL

Just about safe

Hazardous

Scary

Life threatening

F***** ME!!!!

Sentencing recommendation:

If this is the best that God's own county can offer to the cyclist, then REGIME CHANGE is definitely in order.

CRAP CYCLE LANES

OLYMPIC TIN

Cycling competitors in the 2012 Olympics will have World-class training opportunities, right here on the East London streets. On the pavements, in fact.

After a few days of bunny-hopping from one 30cm square to the next, bouncing straight over litter bins from a standing start, and landing with the back wheel down on the next little square, a place on the winners podium will be a breeze to attain.

DIFFICULTY

What a jape it will be, springing between the jolly local cockerknees. Who says we lack facilities to develop the talents of our eager, budding athletes?

DANGER LEVEL

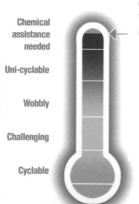

Chemical assistance needed

Uni-cyclable

Wobbly

Challenging

Cyclable

Just about safe

Hazardous

Scary

Life threatening

F**** ME!!!!

Sentencing recommendation:

The streets of the Olympic Village will be seen by visitors from all over the world, or so Ken would have us believe. Newham Council; you deserve at least an ASBO

CRAP CYCLE LANES

CYCLE PARKING

The large supermarket chains see cyclists as a healthy market, and they will go to endless lengths to welcome us. Nothing is too much trouble for them. Cycle parking, sir?

Tesco offer this custom-designed, er, pole. Bring a friend. Bring all your friends… wait, no. Better just bring one friend. Otherwise you might have to start piling the bikes on top of each other, and it could get a bit wrinkly if someone wanted to get their bike out from the bottom, whilst you are still pondering between the pecorino and the Parmigiano Reggiano at the deli counter.

And you can do it where they've B&Q'd it. The store inside is full of tools, so just pop in for a pipe-wrench, and bend your wheels to fit this handy facility.

DIFFICULTY

Chemical
assistance
needed

Uni-cyclable

Wobbly

Challenging

Cyclable

DANGER LEVEL

Just about safe

Hazardous

Scary

Life threatening

F**** ME!!!!

Sentencing recommendation:

Well, there is a simple answer for this, and all of the comparable facilities that you encounter in shopping centres: shop elsewhere. That does leave the offending merchants with the all-time, all-purpose sloppy trader's excuse; 'There's no demand, guv.' We recommend; TAGGING AND A CURFEW

TAKE IT TO THE BANK

Security is the catch-all excuse for any and all kinds of witless impediments on the streets of London. This happens more in the Square Mile – the City of London – than anywhere else.

Here, with a lovely view of the Guildhall, is an excellent ride of about 3 meters, all the way from the kerb to the traffic lights.

Concrete tank-traps offer a thrilling peek-a-boo chicken run across Cannon Street.

And handsome, squared and ribbed bollards in Finsbury square can re-style your wheels, adjust your pedals, or easily add a whole new range of motion to your knees.

DIFFICULTY

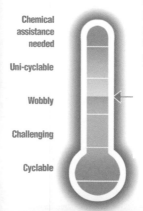

Chemical assistance needed

Uni-cyclable

Wobbly

Challenging

Cyclable

DANGER LEVEL

Just about safe

Hazardous

Scary

Life threatening

F**** ME!!!!

Sentencing recommendation:

A vast proportion of the wealth of the Western world sloshes around the precincts of the City. Not only that, but many of the masters of the universe who earn big enough bonuses to buy small countries as birthday presents actually cycle to work. We recommend a CUSTODIAL SENTENCE

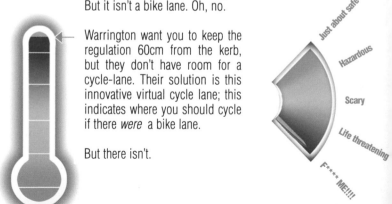

NOW YOU SEE IT...

CRAP CYCLE LANES

A challenge, above and beyond the usual obstacle courses and hazard negotiation that confront cyclists on lesser bike lanes. Warrington like to present logical puzzles, brain teasers bordering in this case on the philosophical.

To paraphrase the great Belgian surrealist, René Magritte, *Ceci n'est pas un cycle-lane.*

DIFFICULTY

It looks like a bike lane, oh, yes. It has the painted bike that you *think* announces a bike lane, oh, yes. But it isn't a bike lane. Oh, no.

Warrington want you to keep the regulation 60cm from the kerb, but they don't have room for a cycle-lane. Their solution is this innovative virtual cycle lane; this indicates where you should cycle if there *were* a bike lane.

But there isn't.

DANGER LEVEL

Chemical assistance needed

Uni-cyclable

Wobbly

Challenging

Cyclable

Just about safe

Hazardous

Scary

Life threatening

F**** ME!!!!

Sentencing recommendation:

There's no excuse for this baffling non-provision of a cycle lane, and only one possible recommendation for us to make: REGIME CHANGE

REGIME CHANGE

CRAP CYCLE LANES

IS IT A BIRD? IS IT A PLANE? NO…
IT'S A CAR

This example from Wigan shows a planning mentality which flirts daintily along the fringes of criminal stupidity. There are clearly at least two visible likelihoods of pedal and motor traffic collisions, due to inspirational planning processes.

Handy for the shops, though, so that's nice.

DIFFICULTY

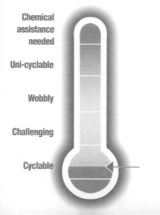

Chemical assistance needed

Uni-cyclable

Wobbly

Challenging

Cyclable

DANGER LEVEL

Just about safe

Hazardous

Scary

Life threatening

F**** ME!!!!

Sentencing recommendation:

This is an example of box-ticking narrow mindedness at its very worst. Only one sentence can be appropriate here, and we commend it to the cycling electorate; REGIME CHANGE

REGIME CHANGE

CENTRAL RESERVATION (FOR BIKES)

To the untrained eye, it looks as though a cycle path has been set among the outer lanes of motor traffic, far from any emergency refuge or safe opportunities for lane or course change.

Fortunately, all British car, bus and lorry drivers think out and plan their lane positions and choices well in advance, indicating clearly and in good time, and manoeuvring only when they are certain that all road users understand their intentions.

DIFFICULTY

As we know, British drivers rarely, if ever, make sudden, screeching, unpredictable swerves a few feet before a junction, intersection or route divergence.

The exhaustive study that went into planning this cycle lane was undertaken by a consortium of Tinkerbell and the Tooth Fairy, using bespoke Magic Bean analysis.

DANGER LEVEL

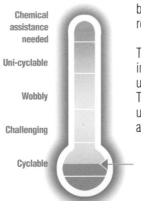

Chemical assistance needed

Uni-cyclable

Wobbly

Challenging

Cyclable

Just about safe

Hazardous

Scary

Life threatening

F***** ME!!!!

Sentencing recommendation:

This would be the kind of thing to get traffic planners a bad name, if they had a good name to start with. Why doesn't town road planning command greater respect, we wonder? We recommend a CUSTODIAL SENTENCE

CRAP CYCLE LANES

SCRATCH & SNIFF

CRAP CYCLE LANES

The sign blowing the logo-ego trumpets of the wonderful folks without whom it would never have been possible takes up almost as much space as the cycle lane itself. It probably cost about as much to make and install, too.

Come to sunny Cambridgeshire and enjoy a magnificent whiz along the superb blink-and-you'll-miss-them bicycle facilities.

DIFFICULTY

Maybe that's the cunning plan – not so much a bike lane, more a subliminal advertising innovation.

What a good thing the Fens Cycle Tourism Project has its priorities so well sorted out.

DANGER LEVEL

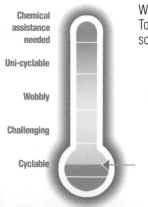

Chemical assistance needed

Uni-cyclable

Wobbly

Challenging

Cyclable

Just about safe

Hazardous

Scary

Life threatening

F***** ME!!!!

Sentencing recommendation:

The CEO of every organisation trumpeted in this bit of self-serving highway puff should be publicly served an ASBO

PARK & RIDE - SIMULTANEOUSLY

Systems like this are excellent for cycling right into cars, as their doors are flung open, and give innumerable opportunities to test your reflexes, as you swerve to avoid happy shoppers swinging their Chelsea tractors at you.

The best fun, though, is to be had by riding the pitch-and-yaw obstacle course, straight over the parked vehicles.

DIFFICULTY

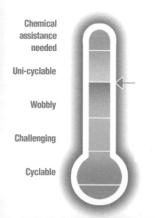

Chemical
assistance
needed

Uni-cyclable

Wobbly

Challenging

Cyclable

DANGER LEVEL

Just about safe

Hazardous

Scary

Life threatening

F***** ME!!!!

Sentencing recommendation:

Warrington have provided so many examples of
the misuse of cycle lane funding, we cannot
make any recommendation other than a
maximum shock 'n' awe delivery of; REGIME
CHANGE

MERRY-GO-ROUND

Here's a delightful way to wile away endless hours, cycling in circles by leafy corners. English Partnerships have innovated dozens of these little gems.

Approaching a big bend or complicated junction and feeling apprehensive? No problem; just take a little left, turn back on yourself, and take another run up at it.

DIFFICULTY Still not quite steeled for the junction? Just hack across the traffic, and head back for home. **DANGER LEVEL**

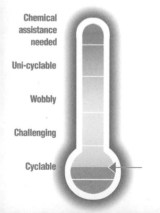

Chemical assistance needed

Uni-cyclable

Wobbly

Challenging

Cyclable

Just about safe

Hazardous

Scary

Life threatening

F**** ME!!!!

Sentencing recommendation:

What should we do with English Partnerships? This is obviously a way to eke out that pesky cycle-lane funding, and every time they write a report, they can cite the combined length of these tracks, and appear to have done something useful. Actually, they're slightly less useful than handles on an ice-cream. We recommend; TAGGING AND A CURFEW

ON-ROAD DIRT TRACK

We all know that feeling. There you are, whizzing along a shared use cycle lane, traffic breezing by on your right, but, oops – here comes a left turn. You don't want to turn off, but the cars might.

What you need is a minute turn-off you can swerve into, and a little plastic bollard you can cower behind, until the nasty broom-brooms have all gone by.

Magic. And look at the lovely landscaping.

DIFFICULTY

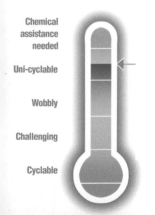

- Chemical assistance needed
- Uni-cyclable
- Wobbly
- Challenging
- Cyclable

DANGER LEVEL

- Just about safe
- Hazardous
- Scary
- Life threatening
- F**** ME!!!!

Sentencing recommendation:

The breathtaking, muddle-headed idiocy of this
facility certainly merits an ASBO

BIKE LANE FOR MINI-ME

Nottingham City Council have provided this marvel in miniature. A two-way cycle track has been painstakingly micro-engineered onto the outside of the pedestrian space.

It works perfectly, just as long as cyclists in opposite directions plan ahead, to ensure that they fit different height handlebars.

Pedestrians too can be quite comfortable, walking in single file, and the council have given them plenty of room to carry shopping as wide as, say, a magazine.

Not a thick magazine, obviously, but if you wanted to read Christmas issues of Vogue or Vanity Fair, surely you wouldn't live in Nottingham. Or so the council would seem to assume.

DIFFICULTY

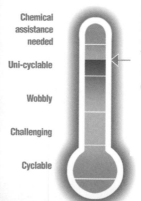

Chemical assistance needed

Uni-cyclable

Wobbly

Challenging

Cyclable

DANGER LEVEL

Just about safe

Hazardous

Scary

Life threatening

F**** ME!!!!

Sentencing recommendation:

Some mitigation must be allowed here for the quaint model-railway approach. The cycle lane would only work for scale model bicycles, and if you tried to steer a real bike within the markings, somebody would certainly get hurt so, we recommend a CUSTODIAL SENTENCE

BUNNY-HOPS

CRAP CYCLE LANES

Planning bike lanes is obviously a task that demands strict professional standards, and the ability to use very precise, and small, units of measurement.

Gateshead have applied themselves vigorously to the stringent task, and haven't wasted any of the precious millimetres at their disposal. Barely the width of a BMX tyre, this cycle lane is equally demanding of cyclists, particularly for the angelic 20-foot leaps required at each bus stop.

Bravo, Gateshead, truly the angels of the North.

DIFFICULTY

DANGER LEVEL

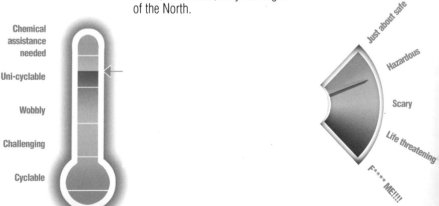

Chemical assistance needed

Uni-cyclable

Wobbly

Challenging

Cyclable

Just about safe

Hazardous

Scary

Life threatening

F**** ME!!!!

Sentencing recommendation:

We believe that, for these absurdly taxing
facilities, Gateshed's parsimonious tarmac
allocation is worthy of an ASBO

CRAP CYCLE LANES

CRAP CYCLE LANES

Marvellously lit at both ends, as the picture shows, Manchester have gone to a great deal of trouble and expense to construct this sumptuous sports cycle track.

Endlessly popular with riders who race the length-and-a-quarter, turn, and race back again. From the middle of nowhere to somewhere very, very near the middle of nowhere.

DIFFICULTY   This facility is a strong contender for our special, 'what the f*** were they thinking of?' award.   **DANGER LEVEL**

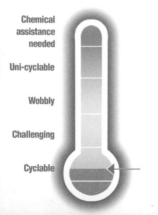

Chemical
assistance
needed

Uni-cyclable

Wobbly

Challenging

Cyclable

Just about safe

Hazardous

Scary

Life threatening

F***** ME!!!!

Sentencing recommendation:

Well, no-one is likely to get hurt on this facility, other than by cyclists spinning their bikes around at either end, so perhaps Manchester would wake their ideas up a little, and benefit from a CAUTION

CAUTION

CRAP CYCLE LANES

"BIKES? I SEE NO BIKES"

The imaginative interpretation of road safety needs that led to cycle lanes against the flow of traffic, is creatively extended into purposefully directing pedestrians to look away from the oncoming cyclists, in the maritime borough of Greenwich.

Be careful not to break the spell by ringing a bell, or by casting amiable taunts at the people, as they step off the kerb with their backs to you.

DIFFICULTY

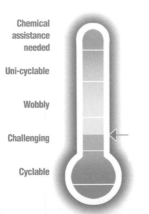

Chemical assistance needed

Uni-cyclable

Wobbly

Challenging

Cyclable

DANGER LEVEL

Just about safe

Hazardous

Scary

Life threatening

F***** ME!!!!

Sentencing recommendation:

Apart from the most attractive remedy, which would be to compel Greenwich Councillors to spend a number of days taking turns to follow the pedestrian directions, and then to pedal the cycle-lane. Failing that, we recommend **TAGGING AND A CURFEW**

RURAL RIDDLE

CRAP CYCLE LANES

After a quick hop up onto the pavement, cyclists are considerably catered to by the right-hand side marking, steering bikes away from that awkward slopey edge of the pavement. Having half of the bike lane suddenly occupied by a tree seems an unwelcome surprise, though.

Perhaps that would be why a kind operative of the highways department has tied warning traffic cones together, and placed them either side of the arboreal encroachment.

This must be what Lincoln planners understand 'joined-up thinking' to mean - thinking about things for a bit, and then tying them together.

DIFFICULTY

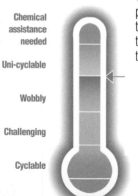

Chemical assistance needed

Uni-cyclable

Wobbly

Challenging

Cyclable

DANGER LEVEL

Just about safe

Hazardous

Scary

Life threatening

F**** ME!!!!

Sentencing recommendation:

All the hearts involved in this facility seem to be in roughly the right place, it's just the eyeballs and brains that seem to be lolling aimlessly. We recommend a CAUTION

PLAY CHICKEN WITH CONCRETE

What could Breckland District Council have actually intended for cyclists to do in the left-hand side of this bike path? Were they really hoping for one to swing a cycle over the bollard at the start, turn the pedals one and a half times, thwack smartly into a post of resilient concrete, and then leave, taking, presumably, a salutary lesson of some kind?

Other than the lesson the front wheel would long remember, that is. The most puzzling aspect of this very baffling arrangement is, why do cyclists coming the other way not benefit from any similar special arrangements?

DIFFICULTY

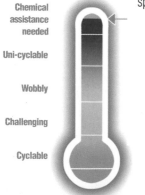

Chemical
assistance
needed

Uni-cyclable

Wobbly

Challenging

Cyclable

DANGER LEVEL

Just about safe

Hazardous

Scary

Life threatening

F***** ME!!!!

Sentencing recommendation:

Breckland District Council have produced the only bike lane so far on our list to be literally cruel and undeniably unusual, in other words, it meets the definition of torture in the Geneva Convention. We recommend immediate REGIME CHANGE

REGIME CHANGE

CRAP CYCLE LANES

IT'S A LANE OF TWO HALVES

North Bridge Road must have posed a field-strength test for Doncaster highways committee's *Head and Shoulders*. The result is a faultless example of clarity in street marking, and in confidence of purpose.

Note the generous width of the cycle lane, and it hasn't been achieved by squeezing the vehicle carriageways. This attention to detail is touching. Particularly so when you consider that the road is closed to traffic.

All it lacks is a footbridge, for the pedestrians to cross over the cyclepath.

DIFFICULTY

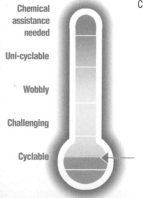

Chemical assistance needed

Uni-cyclable

Wobbly

Challenging

Cyclable

DANGER LEVEL

Just about safe

Hazardous

Scary

Life threatening

F**** ME!!!!

Sentencing recommendation:

Once you've teleported yourself and your bike to the start of this bike lane, it's wide, clearly marked and, just a little bit *anally retentive* in it's layout. There isn't anything really *wrong* with it, it's just rather pointless. We think, for this one, a CAUTION would suffice.

PLAY CHICKEN WITH BUSES

On this cycle lane, Coventry City Council have made provision for you to slip out from under the bus, onto a thoughtfully provided pavement refuge, safe from the motor traffic. In the other direction, you can nip off the cycle track and, again, straight under the bus. Or you may prefer to dice with the oncoming vehicles.

DIFFICULTY

Chemical
assistance
needed

Uni-cyclable

Wobbly

Challenging

Cyclable

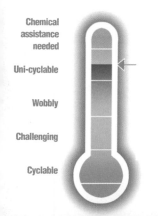

DANGER LEVEL

Just about safe

Hazardous

Scary

Life threatening

F**** ME!!!!

Sentencing recommendation:

How do city councils arrive at locations for the beginnings and ends of bike lanes? Is it through a variation of blind planners bluff? We recommend a CUSTODIAL SENTENCE

THE END IS (VERY) NIGH

Another well-signposted, but abrupt end to a part of the National Cycle Network. This part is on Route 72, on Newtown Road in Carlisle. From this point, you must take up thy cycle and walk. Forgive the pedantry, but doesn't the word 'Network' carry an implication of connectedness?

DIFFICULTY

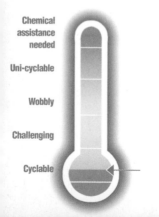

Chemical
assistance
needed

Uni-cyclable

Wobbly

Challenging

Cyclable

DANGER LEVEL

Just about safe

Hazardous

Scary

Life threatening

F**** ME!!!!

Sentencing recommendation:

This is yet another example of cycle-lane provision by the box-ticking bean counter method. We recommend an ASBO

IT'S GOOD TO TALK

The question here is; which is the chicken, and which is the egg.

Did BT have the brilliant idea to site a phone box in the middle of a cycle lane, to attract sackloads of coin revenue from cyclists inspired by the very sight of a callbox to phone home, or call ahead, or just to stop and call their mums?

Or, did the local authority for North Harrow hit on the inspiration to run teeny strips of bike lane either side of an existing phone box, to lend a sense of danger to pedestrians trying to make a call?

DIFFICULTY

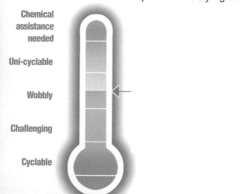

Chemical
assistance
needed

Uni-cyclable

Wobbly

Challenging

Cyclable

DANGER LEVEL

Just about safe

Hazardous

Scary

Life threatening

F**** ME!!!!

Sentencing recommendation:

For this masterpiece in flateral thinking, we
recommend an ASBO

ASBO

CRAP CYCLE LANES

A RUBBISH BIKE LANE

What to do with all that waste paper that you always accumulate whizzing along the superb cycle paths of England. It's a constant worry, and Brent Council have come up with a solution. Not only is there a handy disposal point for the packaging from all the shopping that you just can't wait to get home and unwrap, but right afterwards is the tightest of chicanes around a nice, grey, steel pole.

DIFFICULTY

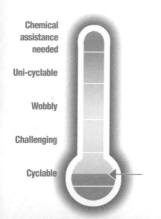

Chemical assistance needed

Uni-cyclable

Wobbly

Challenging

Cyclable

DANGER LEVEL

Just about safe

Hazardous

Scary

Life threatening

F**** ME!!!!

Sentencing recommendation:

The cycle lane here is clearly a lower priority than the litter bin, and its location, barely a meter from the lamppost shows an unmistakable disinterest in the comfort or safety of cyclists. We recommend a CUSTODIAL SENTENCE

CRAP CYCLE LANES

COVENTRY VELODROME

Coventry City Council have taken a clear lead, in being one of the only local authorities to have grasped the appeal of very, very short distance cycling as a spectator sport. This intimate, sheltered grandstand will, no doubt, soon be thronged with food stalls, a bar, and t-shirt, poster and CD sellers, both official and pirate. Watch out for ticket touts.

DIFFICULTY

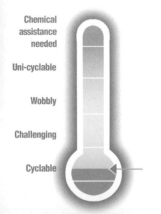

Chemical
assistance
needed

Uni-cyclable

Wobbly

Challenging

Cyclable

DANGER LEVEL

Just about safe

Hazardous

Scary

Life threatening

F**** ME!!!!

Sentencing recommendation:

What we'd like most is a 450-500 word essay on 'why I built this cycle lane.' Our second choice would be to award a few goes on a ducking stool. Failing that, we recommend an ASBO

BICYCLE LEAP-FROG

National Cycle Network route 21 is very well marked on this friendly bollard, and if you approach it at any speed, you can have it embossed on your groin as a commemorative indentation. It makes a great talking point, just the thing to break the ice when meeting new people. Take some ice when you go to get your impression made, as it will smart for a few days afterwards.

DIFFICULTY

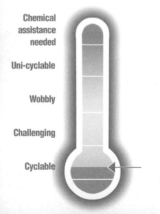

Chemical
assistance
needed

Uni-cyclable

Wobbly

Challenging

Cyclable

DANGER LEVEL

Just about safe

Hazardous

Scary

Life threatening

F**** ME!!!!

Sentencing recommendation:

Kent County Council are taking the National
Cycle Network so seriously that they're ready to
injure users to mark it. The zealotry gains our
recommendation of a CUSTODIAL SENTENCE

CRAP CYCLE LANES

THE BLACKPOOL DODGEMS

The lane markings are pretty explicit here. Blackpool Council can't be faulted for the clarity of this bike path. Cycle within a one meter space, do not deviate right or left, and smack your bars and knuckles into a lamppost at roughly fifty meter intervals. It gives a journey rhythm.

DIFFICULTY

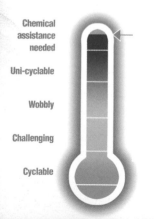

Chemical assistance needed

Uni-cyclable

Wobbly

Challenging

Cyclable

DANGER LEVEL

Just about safe

Hazardous

Scary

Life threatening

F**** ME!!!!

Sentencing recommendation:

Blackpool don't deserve cyclists. That's all
there is to it. We recommend REGIME CHANGE

CRAP CYCLE LANES

COMPLY IF YOU CAN

Solid white lines indicate a mandatory cycle lane, which motor vehicles are forbidden to enter, As we can see, exemplary compliance from local drivers keeps the lane clear of parked cars for its entire length. Well done all.

DIFFICULTY

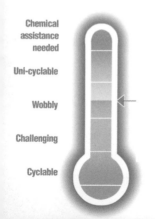

Chemical assistance needed

Uni-cyclable

Wobbly

Challenging

Cyclable

DANGER LEVEL

Just about safe

Hazardous

Scary

Life threatening

F**** ME!!!!

Sentencing recommendation:

Perhaps this cycle facility was last on the order of Oxford Council's business after a difficult Friday afternoon. The phrase, 'must try harder' springs to mind. We recommend an ASBO

IDLE RECREATION

The barriers that Sheffield City have erected at the end of this cycle path, along with the clear, 'cyclists dismount' signs, will certainly keep cyclists safe from straying onto the dual carriageway. So that's a relief. The perennial question remains, though, 'is your journey really necessary?' Sheffield councillors shouldn't think us ungrateful, but there doesn't seem to be anywhere very much to go. Perhaps we ask too much for recreation.

DIFFICULTY

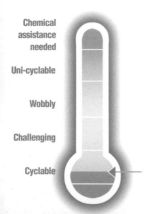

Chemical assistance needed

Uni-cyclable

Wobbly

Challenging

Cyclable

DANGER LEVEL

Just about safe

Hazardous

Scary

Life threatening

F***** ME!!!!

Sentencing recommendation:

Sheffield City Council have provided everything
a cycle lane should be; it's safe, segregated
from traffic, it could be more clearly marked but
it's unmistakably a bike lane, so what more
could one possibly ask. How about cycle lanes
that go from somewhere, and to somewhere?
We recommend a CUSTODIAL SENTENCE

ROUND T' BEND

This little piece of pavement right at the apex of this curve on this Mill Forest Road junction is most likely sacred to one of the local faith communities. Or maybe it has been chosen to represent Batley in the 'little bit of pavement tarmac with the least bicycle tyre rubber in Yorkshire,' award. Either way, the taxing swerve through these brambles and shaggy hedges is a bracing alert for bare shins.

DIFFICULTY

Chemical assistance needed

Uni-cyclable

Wobbly

Challenging

Cyclable

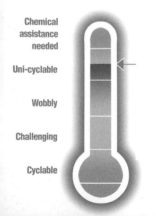

DANGER LEVEL

Just about safe

Hazardous

Scary

Life threatening

F**** ME!!!!

Sentencing recommendation:

Yorkshire folk pride themselves on plain speaking. This bike lane is good fer nowt, and tha must be soft in't head. We recommend an ASBO

CRAP CYCLE LANES

A-MAZE

Cycle-calming measures are springing up all over the country, but this one in the Wirral shows an uncommon degree of ingenuity. It is second to none in robust engineering, nor in complexity.

The purpose is rather harder to discern, though. Is this intricate stile meant to regulate the speed of foot traffic by the height of the pedestrians, or is the Wirral plagued by stampeding Rhinos?

DIFFICULTY

Whatever the intent, the two shorter barriers are guaranteed to rearrange your pedals into an intriguing new shape.

DANGER LEVEL

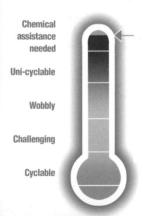

Chemical assistance needed

Uni-cyclable

Wobbly

Challenging

Cyclable

Just about safe

Hazardous

Scary

Life threatening

F**** ME!!!!

Sentencing recommendation:

Perhaps the Wirral had some rejected pieces left over from a competition to design playground equipment. Or perhaps one of the councillors doodled on the plans. Whatever. We recommend a CUSTODIAL SENTENCE

STRADDLE THE FENCE

Two-way cycle lanes can be hazardous, especially where the width is tight. That danger of collision is ever-present. Coventry City Council have banished the risk altogether with this innovative segregating fence.

See, also, how the metal sign at the far end of the fence gives a subtle reminder to cyclists of the value of a second knee, and the need to keep knees and feet a good distance from the centre of the facility.

DIFFICULTY

Notice also how the advanced cycling option of riding along the top of the fence is safely restricted to one-way riding by the top bars of the fence being staggered.

DANGER LEVEL

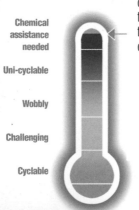

Chemical assistance needed

Uni-cyclable

Wobbly

Challenging

Cyclable

Just about safe

Hazardous

Scary

Life threatening

F**** ME!!!!

Sentencing recommendation:

The reward for this mushy pea-brained thinking should be nothing short of a **CUSTODIAL SENTENCE**

BIN THERE

Warrington Borough Council are far-sighted and pro-active about the needs of cyclists. Thoughtfully camouflaged, so as not to distract a rider's concentration, and carefully leaned 'Tower of Pisa'-style, to accommodate bikes leaning into the curve, this handy litter bin is ideal for dropping off energy drinks bottles, sweet wrappers and surplus ironmongery. See how neatly it divides the cycle path, too.

This pic also has the honour of inspiring the Warrington Cycle Campaign's *Cycle Facility of the Month* feature on their estimable website.

DIFFICULTY

Chemical assistance needed
Uni-cyclable
Wobbly
Challenging
Cyclable

DANGER LEVEL

Just about safe
Hazardous
Scary
Life threatening
F**** ME!!!!

Sentencing recommendation:

Warrington Borough Council really ought to get the appreciation and recognition that they deserve for this masterpiece in cycle path provision. We recommend REGIME CHANGE

CRAP CYCLE LANES

eye**Sight**

'Our greatest fear is not that we are inadequate, our greatest fear is that we are powerful beyond measure. By shining your light, you subconsciously give permission to others to shine theirs.'
Nelson Mandela

Travel can be a liberating experience. As it was for me in 1990, when I was just one hundred yards from Nelson Mandela as he was released from prison. I watched this monumental occasion from on top of a traffic light, amidst a sea of enthralled onlookers.

This was the 'green light' moment that inspired the creation of Eye Books. From the chaos of that day arose an appreciation of the opportunities that the world around us offers, and the desire within me to shine a light for those whose reaction to opportunity is 'can't and don't'.

Our world has been built on dreams, but the drive is often diluted by the corporate and commercial interests offering to live those dreams for us, through celebrity culture and the increasing mechanisation and automation of our lives. Inspiration comes now from those who live outside our daily routines, from those who challenge the way we see things.

Eye Books was born to tell the stories of 'ordinary' people doing 'extraordinary' things. With no experience of publishing, or the constraints that the book 'industry' imposes, Eye Books created a genre of publishing to champion those who live out their dreams.

Ten years on, and sixty stories later Eye Books has the same ethos. We believe that ethical publishing matters. It is not about just trying to make a quick hit, it is about publishing the stories that affect our lives and the lives of others positively. We publish the books we believe will shine a light on the lives of some and enlighten the lives of many for years to come.

Join us in the community of Eye Books, and share the power these stories evoke.

Dan Hiscocks
Founder and Publisher

eye books

At Eye Books we are constantly challenging the way we see things and do things. But we cannot do this alone. To that end we have created an online club, a community, where members can inspire and be inspired, share knowledge and exchange ideas.

eye**Community**

Membership is free, and you can join by visiting www.eye-books.com, where you will be able to find:

What we publish
Books that truly inspire, by people who have given their all, triumphed over adversity, lived their lives to the full.
Visit the dedicated microsites we have for each of our books online.

Why we publish
To champion those 'ordinary' people doing extraordinary things. The real celebrities of our world who tell stories that celebrate life to the full, not just for 15 minutes.
Books where fact is more compelling than fiction.

How we publish
Eye Books is committed to ethical publishing. Many of our books feature and campaign for various good causes and charities.
We try to minimise our carbon footprint in the manufacturing and distribution of our books.

Who we publish
Many, indeed most of our authors have never written a book before. Many start as readers and club members. If you feel strongly that you have a book in you, and it is a book that is experience driven, inspirational and life affirming, visit the 'How to Become an Author' page on our website. We are always open to new authors.

eye**Community**

Eye-Books.com Club is an ever evolving community, as it should be, and benefits from all that our members contribute.

eye-**Books Club** membership offers you:

eye-**News** – a regular emailed newsletter of events in our community.

Special offers and discounts on the books we publish.

Invitations to book launches, signings and author talks.

Correspond with Eye Books authors, directly. About writing, about their books, or about trips you may be planning.

Each month, we receive enquiries from people who have read our books, entered our competitions or heard of us through the media or from friends, people who have a common desire — to make a difference with their lives, however big or small, and to extend the boundaries of everyday life and to learn from others' experiences.

The Eye Books Club is here to support our members, and we want to encourage you to participate. As we all know, the more you put into life, the more you get out of it.

Eye Books membership is free, and it's easy to sign up. Visit our website. Registration takes less than a minute.

eyeBookshelf

	The Good Life *Dorian Amos*	The Good Life Gets Better *Dorian Amos*	Cry From the Highest Mountain *Tess Burrows*	Riding the Outlaw Trail *Simon Casson & Richard Adamson*	Trail of Visions Route 2 *Vicki Couchman*	Riding with Ghosts *Gwen Maka*	South of the Border *Gwen Maka*	Lost Lands Forgotten Stories *Alexandra Pratt*	Frigid Women *Sue and Victoria Riches*	Touching Tibet *Niema Ash*	First Contact *Mark Anstice*	Tea for Two *Polly Benge*	Baghdad Business School *Heynrick Bond Gunning*
eye**Thinker**	•	•	•		•		•	•		•	•	•	•
eye**Adventurer**	•	•		•		•	•	•	•		•	•	•
eye**Quirky**					•								
eye**Cyclist**						•	•					•	
eye**Rambler**													
eye**Gift**					•								
eye**Spiritual**													
				THE AMERICAS							**ASIA**		

www.eye-books.com

eye**Bookshelf**

Title / Author	eye**Thinker**	eye**Adventurer**	eye**Quirky**	eye**Cyclist**	eye**Rambler**	eye**Gift**	eye**Spiritual**	Region
Jungle Janes — *Peter Burden*		•						ASIA
Trail of Visions — *Vicki Couchman*	•	•				•		ASIA
Desert Governess — *Phyllis Ellis*	•		•					ASIA
Fever Trees of Borneo — *Mark Eveleigh*		•						ASIA
My Journey with a Remarkable Tree — *Ken Finn*	•							ASIA
The Jungle Beat — *Roy Follows*	•	•						ASIA
Siberian Dreams — *Andy Home*	•	•						ASIA
Behind the Veil — *Lydia Laube*		•						ASIA
Good Morning Afghanistan — *Waseem Mahmood*	•	•						ASIA
Jasmine and Arnica — *Nicola Naylor*	•							ASIA
Prickly Pears of Palestine — *Hilda Reilly*	•	•						ASIA
Last of the Nomads — *W J Peasley*								AUS
Travels in Outback Australia — *Andrew Stevenson*	•							AUS

www.eye-books.com

eyeBookshelf

	Green Oranges on Lion Mountain — Emily Joy	Zohra's Ladder — Pamela Windo	Walking Away — Charlotte Metcalf	Changing the World One Step at a Time — Michael Meegan	All Will Be Well — Michael Meegan	Seeking Sanctuary — Hilda Reilly	Crap Cycle Lanes — Captain Yellowjersey	50 Quirky Bike Rides...in England and Wales — Rob Ainsley	On the Wall with Hadrian — Bob Bibby	Special Offa — Bob Bibby	The European Job — Jonathan Booth	Fateful Beauty — Natalie Hodgson	Slow Winter — Alex Hickman
eyeThinker	•	•	•	•	•	•							•
eyeAdventurer	•							•			•	•	•
eyeQuirky								•			•	•	
eyeCyclist								•					
eyeRambler									•	•			
eyeGift								•					
eyeSpiritual				•		•							

| AFRICA | | | | | | EUROPE | | | | | | | |

www.eye-books.com

eyeBookshelf

	The Accidental Optimist's Guide to Life (Emily Joy)	Con Artist Handbook (Joel Levy)	Forensics Handbook (Pete Moore)	Travels with my Daughter (Niema Ash)	Around the World with 1000 Birds (Russell Boyman)	Death (Herbie Brennan)	Discovery Road (Tim Garratt and Andy Brown)	Great Sects (Adam Hume Kelly)	Triumph Around the World (Robbie Marshall)	Blood Sweat and Charity (Nick Stanhope)	Traveller's Tales from Heaven and Hell (Various)	Further Traveller's Tales from Heaven and Hell (Various)	More Traveller's Tales from Heaven and Hell (Various)
eyeThinker	•	•	•	•		•	•	•					
eyeAdventurer				•		•		•	•	•			
eyeQuirky	•	•	•	•		•		•			•	•	•
eyeCyclist						•							
eyeRambler													
eyeGift		•	•			•		•			•	•	•
eyeSpiritual						•		•					

| EUROPE | | | CROSS CONTINENT | | | | | | | | | | |

www.eye-books.com

eye**Bookshelf**

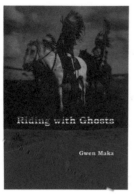

Riding With Ghosts

£7.99

An interest in Native American Indian history and a desire to push herself to the limits sees Gwen (a solo woman) try to bicycle the trail from Seattle to Mexico. Her frank and outrageous account is shared an involvement with the West and it's pioneering past. We almost catch a glimpse of Crazy Horse.

Riding with Ghost - South of the border

£7.99

Having ridden, saddle sore, from Seattle to Mexico, Gwen continued down the America's to San Jose in Costa Rica.
She finds interest in all the pioneers of the South ~ Columbus, Cortes and Montezuma.
She still journeys with abandon and gives the reader a blend of courage, candour and humour.

Tea for two

£7.99

Tim and Polly head to war-torr
follow the 400 mile route taken by the Buddha
over 6 years to enlightenment. They had 6
weeks and two bicycles. They hoped, having
dodged the civil war around them, their love
would stand the strain, moving to the other
side of the world to spend their life together.
Having sold an option for the book to be made
into a film (Bridget Jones goes travelling), it is a
great read for anyone who likes a true love
story.

Discovery Road

£9.99

The first people to mountain bike around the
world. It is a fast moving inspirational tale of self
discovery: full of adventure, conflict, humour,
danger and a multitude of colourful characters.
Much more than a travelogue, it proves that
ordinary people can chase great dreams.

eye**Bookshelf**

Moods of Future Joys

£9.99
46,000 miles, 5 continents, 4 years and only
£7,000 – An old fashioned adventure: long,
lonely, low budget and spontaneous. Two weeks
in and 9/11 forces him to change everything,
but he continues and this is the first part of his
epic trip which Sir Ranulph Fiennes has labelled
'the first great adventure of the new
millennium.'

Thunder & Sunshine

£9.99
Following on from his first best-seller, Alistair
leaves Cape Town wondering whether he will
ever make it home. As he sets sail from South
Africa, he has more than three quarters of the
way left to go. Up through the America's and
Canada and Alaska before crossing through
Asia and Russia, Siberia and back through
Europe. A truly carbon neutral book.

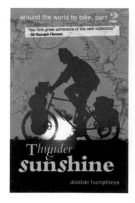

eye**Bookshelf**

50 quirky bike rides

£9.99

A description of 50 quirky things that are uniquely enjoyable by bike: Weird places where you can (metaphorically) take your bike downhill skiing, potholing or tightrope walking, or turn it into a pedalo. Oddities like cycling on a motorway or on the right-hand side of the road. Many can be done in a lunchtime; all make an excuse for a day trip, or a three-month tour.

Blood Sweat & Charity

£9.99

The only charity challenge guidebook to help you through any or all of the process; from identifying the challenge and or the cause to how to document it and maximise the fundraising and awareness whilst making sure that you are physically prepared for whatever you take on.

The Cyclists' Defence Fund

Set up by the CTC, it is now an independent organisation, both a Company Limited by Guarantee and a Registered Charity. CDF is seeking a wider support base, so that it can show support for all cyclists, whether or not they belong to any 'organisation' or club.

Aims:

The Cyclists' Defence Fund works to raise awareness of the law relating to cyclists. Our aims, as formally approved by the Charity Commission, are:

To preserve and protect the health and safety of the public by encouraging and facilitating safe cycling.

To advance the education of the public in the relationship between cycling and the law.

To further the sound development, administration and knowledge of the law relating to cycling.

To promote, assist, undertake and commission research into the law, practice, and administration of justice in connection with cycling and to disseminate the useful results of such research.

We work to achieve these aims in practice by:

Providing guidance on the law relating to cycling and other legal issues with an impact on cyclists.

Maintaining a web-site providing links to legal resources relevant to cycling and cyclists.

Commissioning research into the effectiveness of the legal framework — such research may be useful to cycling campaigners, legislators and others seeking to improve the law.

Providing support in legal cases which could clarify the law.

If you can assist us in any way to achieve these aims please contact the fund.

info@CyclistsDefenceFund.org.uk